Introduction

Welcome to *Illinois Exam Prep*! When you bought this book, you showed that you are serious about passing the exam and getting your real estate license. This is *NOT* an easy test. For people whose test-taking skills are weak, or who haven't adequately prepared, the exam can be a nightmare. For those who have taken the time and effort to study and review, however, the exam can be a much more positive experience.

It's pretty obvious, though, that if you practice and review key material, your test score will improve. This book is your key to exam success.

The process is simple: Just work your way through the practice questions, taking your time and answering each one carefully. Then check your answers by studying the Answer Key, where you'll find both the correct answer to each question as well as an explanation of *why* that answer is correct. It might be a good idea to review your classroom materials and textbook before you start.

Remember: These 200 questions reflect as closely as possible the topic coverage of the state-specific portion of your exam only! For the balance of the test, you'll need to use a "national" exam prep book. And remember, too, that it takes study and hard work on your part to pass the licensing exam: no single study aid will do the trick alone.

Experts who are familiar with the Illinois licensing examination, as well as real estate law and practice, prepared this book. You've taken the first step toward your success as a real estate professional: Good Luck!

Dearborn Real Estate Education

Illinois *Exam Prep*

1. In Illinois, the real estate license law is administered by the

   A. Department of Professional Regulation.
   B. Office of Banks and Real Estate.
   C. Illinois Association of REALTORS®.
   D. Department of Housing and Urban Development.

2. How are members of the Real Estate Administration and Disciplinary Board selected?

   A. By the governor
   B. Public election
   C. By the Illinois Association of REALTORS®
   D. By real estate licensees

3. The Office of Banks and Real Estate may suspend or deny a license for failure to

   A. pay taxes, child support, or any Illinois-guaranteed student loan.
   B. pay child support and properly withhold estimated taxes.
   C. finish a college degree program.
   D. satisfy a disgruntled client.

4. Illinois requires licensees to have which of the following in their possession?

   A. Illinois driver's license
   B. MLS I.D. number
   C. Pocket license card, then a 45-day permit
   D. 45-day sponsor card, then a pocket license card later

5. In Illinois, who of the following would need to be a licensed real estate broker or salesperson?

   A. An apartment manager who manages only 19 units
   B. Licensed attorney acting under a power of attorney to convey real estate
   C. Resident apartment manager working for an owner if the manager's primary residence is the apartment building being managed
   D. Partnership selling a building owned by the partners

6. Which of the following requires a real estate license?

   A. Resident manager who collects rent on behalf of a building owner
   B. Company that matches individuals from different parts of the country who want to exchange properties for a fee (not a commission).
   C. MLS or other mediums advertising real property
   D. Executor selling a decedent's building

7. An agent holds an open house that a prospect/buyer attends. The agent then shows more listings (not his) to the prospect. Lacking a buyer agency agreement, what is the agent's status if the prospect buys the agent's listing?

   A. Buyer's agent
   B. Dual agent
   C. Seller's agent, performing ministerial acts
   D. Subagent

8. The office coordinator for a local real estate firm is responsible for the following activities: tracking the flow of paperwork through the office, preparing forms and advertising copy, and hiring and supervising clerical personnel. The office coordinator is

   A. violating the license law.
   B. required to have a broker's license.
   C. required to have a salesperson's license.
   D. exempt from real estate licensing requirements.

9. In Illinois, sponsor cards are good for

   A. 45 days.
   B. 60 days.
   C. 180 days.
   D. two years.

10. All of the following are requirements for obtaining a broker's license EXCEPT

    A. having successfully completed 120 hours of approved real estate courses.
    B. being at least 21 years of age.
    C. having been actively engaged as a licensed salesperson for at least one year.
    D. passing the state exam.

11. Buyers properly sign a lead-based paint disclosure form on a house they purchase through a buyer's agent. How long must the buyer's agent keep that signed form?

    A. Until the closing
    B. For three years
    C. For five years
    D. He doesn't need to keep it.

12. A person successfully completed her real estate education requirement on November 1, 2001. What is the latest date on which she may apply for a salesperson's license?

    A. December 1, 2001
    B. November 1, 2003
    C. October 31, 2002
    D. November 1, 2004

13. Three weeks before N begins his real estate prelicense class, he offers to help his neighbor sell her house. The neighbor agrees to pay N a 5 percent commission. An offer is accepted while N is taking the class and closes the day before N passes the examination and receives his salesperson's license. The neighbor refuses to pay N the agreed commission. Can N sue to recover payment?

    A. Yes, because N was formally enrolled in a course of study intended to result in a real estate license at the time an offer was procured and accepted, the commission agreement is binding.
    B. No, in Illinois, a real estate salesperson must have his or her own office in which the sales license is displayed in order to collect a commission from a seller.
    C. Yes, while the statute of frauds forbids recovery on an oral agreement for the conveyance of real property, Illinois law permits enforcement of an oral commission contract under these facts.
    D. No, state law prohibits lawsuits filed to collect commissions unless filed by a licensed broker—one with a license in effect before the agreement was reached.

14. An unlicensed individual who engages in activities for which a real estate license is required is subject to which of the following penalties?

    A. Fine not to exceed $10,000
    B. Fine not to exceed $10,000 and one year imprisonment
    C. Civil penalty of $25,000 in addition to other penalties provided by law
    D. Civil penalty not to exceed $25,000 and a mandatory prison term not to exceed five years

15. When do real estate salespersons' licenses expire in Illinois?

    A. March 31 of every odd-numbered year
    B. June 30 of every even-numbered year
    C. April 30 of every odd-numbered year
    D. January 31 of every odd-numbered year

16. To renew license in Illinois, salespersons or brokers must

    A. only pay a fee of $225.
    B. be actively participating in the real estate business.
    C. have completed six hours of continuing education in the last two years, three hours in real estate law and three hours in fair housing.
    D. have completed 12 hours of CE in the last two years.

17. A licensee who allows his or her license to expire has how long to reinstate the license?

    A. There is no grace period.
    B. Up to two years, then he or she must start over
    C. No more than 30 days
    D. One year from the time it expires

18. Which of the following is an example "ministerial act" under the Illinois agency law?

    A. Arguing the merits of an offer on behalf of a prospective buyer
    B. Helping prospective buyers determine an appropriate price range and geographical location for their home search
    C. Responding to general questions about the price and location of a specific property
    D. Assisting a buyer in asking for repairs (to be made by seller) after a home inspection

19. Services performed for a buyer that do not create an agency relationship are referred to as

    A. transactional acts.
    B. routine brokerage.
    C. ministerial acts.
    D. vicarious subagency.

20. In Illinois, an unlicensed real estate assistant may perform all of the following activities EXCEPT

   A. compute commission checks.
   B. assemble legal documents required for a closing.
   C. explain simple contract documents to prospective buyers. *(circled)*
   D. prepare and distribute flyers and promotional materials.

21. In Illinois, a personal real estate assistant

   A. must be licensed.
   B. may insert factual information into forms under the agent's supervision and approval. *(circled)*
   C. may host open houses and home show booths.
   D. must be unlicensed; licenses are only required of salespeople or brokers.

22. An agent has had a listing for a year. An agent from another office has shown it several times to a prospective buyer, but the prospect cannot make an offer until their house sells. The first agent's listing expires, and the second agent gets the listing. If the prospective buyer purchases it during the first agent's protection period, is the first agent entitled to any commission?

   A. Yes, the first agent is entitled to the original commission split.
   B. Yes, but the first agent will have to split the listing fee with the second agent
   C. No, the first agent will get nothing.
   D. No, but the first agent should ask the second agent for a referral fee

23. The broker's unlicensed assistant worked late nights and weekends to help ensure the successful closing of a difficult transaction. The assistant's extra work included making several phone calls to the prospective buyers, encouraging them to accept the seller's counteroffer. Largely because of the assistant's efforts, the sale went through with no problem. Now the broker wants to pay the assistant a percentage of the commission "because the assistant has really earned it." Under Illinois law, the broker may

   A. compensate the assistant in the form of a commission under the circumstances described here.
   B. not pay the assistant a cash commission but is permitted to make a gift of tangible personal property.
   C. not pay a commission to the assistant under the facts presented here. They are both in violation of rules regarding unlicensed assistants.
   D. pay a commission to the assistant only if the assistant is an independent contractor.

24. Which of the following conditions is not required to grant a nonresident license in Illinois?

   A. The agent must have a current license in his or her home state.
   B. The agent must file an irrevocable consent to suit.
   C. The standards for licensing in the agent's home state must be equivalent or greater than those in Illinois.
   D. The OBRE must have a reciprocal agreement with the agent's home state.

25. The on-site property manager for Acme Apartments is responsible for negotiating leases for the apartments. In this position, the on-site manager

    A. must have a salesperson's license.
    B. must have a broker's license.
    C. is exempt from the licensing requirements.
    D. is violating the license law.

26. All of the following are exempt from Illinois licensing requirements EXCEPT a(n)

    A. property owner who sells or leases his or her own property.
    B. individual who receives compensation for procuring prospective buyers or renters of real estate.
    C. individual who is employed as a resident property manager.
    D. resident lessee who receives the equivalent of one month's rent as a "finder's fee" for referring a new tenant to the owner.

27. Which of the following is a requirement to obtain a real estate salesperson's license in Illinois?

    A. Successful completion of 12 credit hours of real estate law, investments, finance, and appraisal
    B. An associate degree or certificate in real estate from an accredited college, university, or proprietary school
    C. United States and Illinois citizenship
    D. Successful completion of a course of 45 classroom, correspondence, or distance learning hours in general principles of real estate

28. What is the expiration date of every broker's license in Illinois?

    A. January 31 of every even-numbered year
    B. April 30 of each even-numbered year
    C. October 31 of each odd-numbered year
    D. April 30 of each odd-numbered year

29. A person must be licensed as a real estate broker or salesperson if that person is

    A. selling her house.
    B. buying a house for her personal use.
    C. engaged in the listing.
    D. constructing houses.

30. In Illinois, all of the following would be grounds for discipline of a broker EXCEPT

    A. being convicted of a felony in Illinois.
    B. advertising in a newspaper that she is a member of the Illinois Association of REALTORS® when she is not.
    C. depositing escrow money in his or her personal checking account.
    D. agreeing with a seller to accept a listing for more than the normal commission rate.

31. The OBRE has the power to discipline a salesperson if the salesperson

    A. fails to make car payments.
    B. attempts to represent a buyer.
    C. enters into an exclusive listing contract.
    D. deposits a buyer's down payment in his or her own bank account.

32. In Illinois, which of the following actions are legal and would not expose a broker to disciplinary action?

   A. Being declared mentally incompetent
   B. Depositing earnest money into the firm's escrow account
   C. Helping another person cheat on the licensing examination
   D. Displaying a "For Sale" sign on a property without the owner's consent

33. All of the following acts would cause licensee to be disciplined by the OBRE EXCEPT

   A. failing to perform as promised in a guaranteed sales plan.
   B. negotiating a very high commission.
   C. commingling others' money or property with her or his own.
   D. failing to provide information requested by the Office of Banks and Real Estate within 24 hours.

34. Under Illinois law, a continuing education instructor receives CE credit

   A. hour-for-hour of each class he or she teaches.
   B. for the first six hours of class he or she teaches.
   C. for elective classes only.
   D. Instructors do not receive CE credit for teaching.

35. Which of the following actions is legal and not a violation of Illinois license law?

   A. Encouraging a seller to reject an offer because the prospective buyer is a Methodist
   B. Placing a "For Sale" sign in front of a house after asking the seller's permission and receiving written permission to go ahead
   C. Advertising that individuals who attend a promotional presentation will receive a prize without mentioning that they will also have to take a day trip to a new subdivision site
   D. Standing in the hallway outside the testing room and offering employment to new licensees as soon as they receive their passing score at the testing center

36. Salesperson J asked the telephone company to list her name in the directory under the "Real Estate" heading as "J, Real Estate Salesperson; residential property is my specialty!" Based on this information, J is also required to include

   A. her license number.
   B. the expiration date of her license.
   C. her street address.
   D. the name of her employing broker.

37. A broker who wishes to place a "For Sale" sign on a property must first

   A. obtain the written consent of the owner of the property.
   B. sell the property.
   C. obtain a building permit.
   D. get permission from the neighbors.

38. When advertising real property, real estate licensees

    A. may state only the licensee's box number or street address.
    B. may give just a telephone number to call for more information.
    C. must indicate the company name of the employing broker.
    D. must identify the owner of the property.

39. A real estate salesperson decides to sell his or her own property without using a broker. When advertising the property, the salesperson

    A. must disclose the name and phone number of his employing broker.
    B. must disclose the fact that she or he is a real estate licensee.
    C. does not need to disclose licensed status if acting as a private citizen.
    D. is prohibited from selling his or her own home in this manner by license law.

40. The broker has developed a web site advertising the broker's office. What, if anything, does the broker need to include?

    A. Name of brokerage and the city and state in which the principal office is located
    B. License number of brokerage and list of current active licensees
    C. Names of active licensees, addresses, and phone numbers
    D. There is no need for any disclosures.

41. A salesperson has developed a web site on the Internet that showcases all his listings. What, if anything, must the salesperson include?

    A. City or geographic area for each property, company name, and state of licensure if property is not within jurisdiction of his license
    B. Name of home office of company that holds his salesperson's license and list of states in which company is licensed
    C. Names of all licensees in broker's office and the states in which they are licensed
    D. There are no disclosures required by Illinois law.

42. Listings based on a "net price" are

    A. more profitable because no minimum is set on the amount of commission collectible.
    B. legal in Illinois as long as the seller agrees.
    C. illegal in Illinois at any time.
    D. permissible with approval of the OBRE.

43. In Illinois, real estate commissions are

    A. set by law.
    B. set by the local MLS.
    C. determined by local groups of brokers.
    D. negotiable between the seller, buyer, and broker.

44. Commissions earned by a broker in a real estate sales transaction

    A. are determined by agreement of the broker and his or her principal.
    B. may be shared with an unlicensed person, provided that such person aided the broker in bringing the buyer and seller together.
    C. may be deducted from the earnest money deposit and claimed by the broker as soon as the buyer and seller execute the purchase and sales agreement.
    D. are based on a schedule of commission rates set by the OBRE.

45. All funds received by a broker on behalf of his or her principal must be deposited in an escrow or trust account within

    A. three days of receiving the offer.
    B. three days of obtaining all signatures for the contract.
    C. five working days of receiving the offer.
    D. one business day of receiving all signatures.

46. If a broker establishes an account to hold money belonging to others, which of the following is correct?

    A. All monies must be held in a federally-insured depository.
    B. Accounts may be interest or non-interest bearing at the direction of the broker.
    C. The account cannot be in the same bank as the broker's personal checking account.
    D. An individual account is required for each transaction.

47. A broker received an earnest money deposit from a buyer. Under Illinois law, the broker should

    A. open a special, separate escrow account that will contain funds for this transaction only, separate from funds received in any other transaction.
    B. deposit the money in an existing special non-interest bearing escrow account in which all earnest money received from buyers may be held at the same time.
    C. immediately (or by the next business day) commingle the funds by depositing the earnest money in the broker's personal interest-bearing checking or savings account.
    D. hold the earnest money deposit in a secure place in the broker's real estate brokerage office until the offer is accepted.

48. In Illinois, brokers and salespeople who are not lawyers may

    A. complete additional documents on the client's behalf after a sales contract has been signed.
    B. fill in blanks on preprinted form contracts customarily used in their community.
    C. suggest additional language to be added to a preprinted sales contract by a buyer or seller.
    D. explain the legal significance of specific preprinted contract clauses to a buyer or seller.

49. All of the following must appear in a written listing agreement EXCEPT

   A. a statement that the property must be shown to all prospective buyers regardless of race, color, religion, national origin, sex, ancestry, marital status, military discharge status, age, handicap, or familial status.
   B. the complete legal description of the property being sold.
   C. the time duration of the listing.
   D. the proposed gross sales price of the property.

50. A broker signs a listing agreement with a seller. The agreement contains this clause: "If the Property has not been sold after three months from date of this signing, this agreement will automatically continue for additional three-month periods until the property sells." Such an agreement

   A. is legal under Illinois law, because it contains a reference to a time limit.
   B. is illegal in Illinois.
   C. automatically receives a statutory six month listing period.
   D. is legal (for periods less than six months each.

51. How many continuing education hours are now required by Illinois license law in each two-year renewal period?

   A. 6 hours of mandatory courses, 6 hours of electives
   B. 6 hours of core courses, 6 hours of electives
   C. 12 hours of core courses
   D. 12 hours of any course

52. Upon obtaining a listing, a broker or licensed salesperson is obligated by Illinois law to

   A. place the property in MLS within 24 hours.
   B. place advertisements in the local newspapers.
   C. cooperate with every real estate office wishing to participate in the marketing of the listed property.
   D. give the person or persons signing the listing a copy within 24 hours.

53. Best Builders and Real Estate, Inc., wishes to offer a new car to anyone purchasing a home priced in excess of $1,000,000. Can they do this under Illinois law?

   A. No, this would be a rebate and is not allowed.
   B. No, this would violate RESPA rules.
   C. Yes, but they must then offer a new car to every home purchaser
   D. Yes, as long as the conditions are spelled out in any ad

54. Upon renewal of his real estate broker's license, a licensee writes a bad check to the OBRE. In this circumstance, the licensee faces

   A. automatically having his license revoked.
   B. paying a $50 fine and the due amount within 30 days or losing his/her license.
   C. paying a $500 fine and then going through the discipline proceedings.
   D. prosecution by the attorney general.

55. A salesperson was engaged in activities violating the Illinois Human Rights Act, including blockbusting and discrimination based on race. The salesperson also failed to complete her continuing education credits and get her license renewed on time. The employing broker claimed to be unaware of all of these activities. What is the impact on the salesperson's broker when these violations are brought to the attention of the OBRE?

    A. The employing broker will not have his or her license disciplined as a result of the salesperson's violations.
    B. The salesperson's employing broker will be required to pay any fine imposed against the salesperson out of his or her own personal funds.
    C. The salesperson's actions are legally the responsibility of the employing broker, who could be penalized if he or she knew, or should have known, of any illegal activities.
    D. The salesperson's employing broker will be held liable for the Human Rights Act violations only.

56. A woman wishes to find a female roommate in order to split the expenses of her two-bedroom, one-bath apartment. Can she indicate "female only" in her newspaper ad?

    A. Yes, sex is not a protected class for rental purposes.
    B. Yes, they have to share one bathroom.
    C. No, you can never discriminate based on sex.
    D. No, you cannot discriminate because the apartment has two bedrooms.

57. If a buyer wants to have a clause included in the sales contract under which the seller offers assurances against the existence of werewolves, vampires, and trolls on the property, which of the following statements is true in Illinois?

    A. The broker may include the clause, because such standard supernatural disclosures are in general usage.
    B. Only a licensed attorney may prepare the clause for inclusion in the sales contract.
    C. In Illinois, brokers are permitted to add additional clauses to blank form contracts, such as the clause described here, that do not directly involve the conveyance of title to real property.
    D. Under Illinois law, a frivolous clause, such as the one described here, is not permitted and any contract containing such a clause will be invalid.

58. An Illinois real estate salesperson may lawfully collect compensation from

    A. either a buyer or a seller.
    B. his or her sponsoring broker only.
    C. any party to the transaction or the party's representative.
    D. a licensed real estate broker only.

59. A salesperson heard that a neighborhood has experienced a large influx of a specific ethnic group. The salesperson then canvasses the neighborhood, urging homeowners to sell before home prices drop. The salesperson is guilty of

    A. steering.
    B. redlining.
    C. antitrust violations.
    D. blockbusting.

60. What are the procedures that a broker must follow when terminating a salesperson?

    A. Give the agent an official letter of termination that he or she can send to the OBRE
    B. Sign the bottom of the agent's license and give to agent, then send a copy to the OBRE and keep one copy on file
    C. Sign the old license and send in original to the OBRE
    D. Sign the old license, file, and give copy to the agent

61. A licensed salesperson may hold a concurrent license with more than one Illinois broker under which of the following circumstances?

    A. Under no circumstances
    B. With the permission of his or her sales manager
    C. With the written consent of the brokers being represented
    D. With the permission of OBRE

62. Several weeks after a closing, a salesperson received a thank-you letter and a nice bonus check from the seller of the house. The salesperson cashed the check because he felt it was earned. In this situation, which statement is true?

    A. The salesperson may accept the bonus if it is not commission.
    B. Accepting the money is allowed if over 30 days have elapsed since the closing.
    C. The salesperson may accept the money if 60 days have passed.
    D. Accepting the money is a violation of OBRE regulations.

63. When a broker/owner has his or her license suspended for two years, what effect does this have on the salespeople affiliated with the proprietor?

    A. Agents' licenses will be revoked, subject to reinstatement after one year.
    B. Agents' licenses will also be suspended for a two-year period.
    C. Suspension has no effect on the agents' licenses.
    D. Agents' licenses are "inoperative" until securing a 45-day sponsor card from a new sponsor.

64. A broker intends to open a branch office in a neighboring town. The broker applies for a branch office license, giving a name that clearly identifies its relationship with his main office. The broker names a licensed real estate salesperson as the branch office manager. Under these facts, will the broker receive approval for the branch office?

    A. Yes, the broker has fully complied with the requirements of the license law.
    B. No, under Illinois license law, brokers cannot have branch offices in more than one municipality.
    C. Yes, by naming the salesperson as the branch's manager, the broker is in compliance with the requirement that a licensee be in charge.
    D. No, the manager of a branch office must be a licensed real estate broker.

65. When a managing broker dies,

   A. the real estate company can no longer exist and all agents must leave.
   B. a sponsoring broker or power of attorney may step in and manage the office temporarily for up to 30 days.
   C. commissions cannot be paid to sales associates for pending sales, as there is no broker.
   D. the OBRE is notified and the office must be immediately closed.

66. In any real estate sales transaction that a broker negotiates, the broker is not required to

   A. inform the buyer of his or her personal opinion of the condition of the seller's title to the property.
   B. make sure that the written purchase and sales agreement includes all the terms of the parties' agreement.
   C. give a copy of the contract to both buyer and seller.
   D. keep copies of all escrow records in his or her files for five years after the transaction was closed.

67. Every Illinois real estate office is required to do all the following EXCEPT

   A. maintain escrow account records for five years.
   B. keep both an escrow journal and ledger.
   C. display signage at the office location.
   D. employ at least one additional salesperson in addition to the broker.

68. An airline pilot told a broker about some friends who were looking for a new home. The broker contacted the friends and eventually sold them a house. When may the broker pay the airline pilot for this valuable lead?

   A. As soon as a valid sales contract is signed by the parties
   B. Only after the sale closes
   C. After the funds are released from escrow
   D. The broker may not pay the pilot for the lead.

69. A broker is convicted on May 1 of embezzlement. Both the crime and the conviction took place out of state. On June 15, the broker calls the OBRE and leaves a message informing the OBRE of the conviction. Based on these facts, which of the following is true?

   A. The broker has properly informed the OBRE within 60 days after the conviction, and the broker's license will be renewed.
   B. Both the conviction and the broker's failure to notify OBRE within 30 days violate OBRE regulations.
   C. Because the conviction did not occur in state, it is not evidence of unworthy conduct.
   D. The conviction may cause the broker to have his or her license suspended or revoked.

70. How is a broker's commission determined in a real estate sales transaction?

   A. It must be stated in the listing agreement and is negotiated between the broker and seller.
   B. It is determined according to the standard rates set by agreement of local real estate brokers.
   C. If under dispute, it will be determined through arbitration by the OBRE.
   D. It must be paid with cash or a cashier's check upon closing.

71. State law requires that an offer to purchase may not be used when it is intended for that form to be a

   A. binding real estate contract.
   B. non-binding contract.
   C. preliminary negotiation form.
   D. standard MLS contract.

72. *Chicago Bar Association, et al v. Quinlan and Tyson, Inc.* established what principle in Illinois real estate law?

   A. Real estate brokers must establish a special escrow account for earnest money deposits.
   B. The seller must bear any losses that occur before title to property passes or before the buyer takes possession.
   C. Brokers and salespersons who are not lawyers may only fill in blanks and make appropriate deletions on preprinted standard form contracts.
   D. Once a contract is signed, a broker or salesperson may not make any additions, deletions, or insertions without the written consent of the parties.

73. A broker wants to list a property but is getting a lot of competition from other brokers who would also like to list it. The broker offers the seller the following inducement to sign his listing agreement: "I'll buy your property if it doesn't sell in 90 days." With this advertising, the broker must do all of the following EXCEPT

   A. buy the property at the agreed figure at any time during the 90 days.
   B. market the property as if no special agreement existed.
   C. show the seller evidence of the broker's financial ability to buy the property.
   D. show the seller details of plan before any guaranty contract is signed.

74. A broker has obtained an offer to purchase a house that is listed with his firm. The buyers sign a purchase and sale agreement and the broker accepts their earnest money deposit. The broker must

   A. deposit the earnest money in the broker's personal checking account for safekeeping until closing.
   B. complete a second earnest money agreement form that states an exaggerated selling price for the buyers to present to the lender so that they will be certain to obtain sufficient financing for their purchase.
   C. provide the buyers a copy of the offer.
   D. file the agreement in the broker's records and, when two or three other offers have been received for the property, present them all to the sellers, who may choose the best one.

75. All of the following agreements must be in writing EXCEPT a(n)

    A. exclusive buyer-agency agreement.
    B. open listing.
    C. exclusive-right-to-sell.
    D. multiple listing.

76. A landlord has a "no pets" policy in his apartment building. If a visually impaired person wants to rent an apartment from the landlord and owns a guide dog, which of the following statements is true?

    A. If the landlord's "no pets" policy is applied consistently in a nondiscriminatory manner, it may be legally applied to a guide dog as well.
    B. The Illinois Human Rights Act specifically prohibits the landlord from refusing to rent the apartment to the visually impaired person on the basis of the owner's "no pets" policy.
    C. Under the Illinois Human Rights Act, the landlord may not discriminate against the visually impaired person on the basis of a "no pets" policy, but the landlord may require the tenant to pay an additional damage fee.
    D. The Illinois Human Rights Act does not address the issue of guide, hearing, or support dogs.

77. In Illinois, the age of legal competence is

    A. 18.
    B. 19.
    C. 20.
    D. 21.

78. All of the following are protected classes under the Illinois Fair Housing Law EXCEPT

    A. race.
    B. handicap.
    C. sexual preference.
    D. national origin.

79. The listing agreement with a seller has expired, and the seller lists with a different firm. The original listing agent now has a buyer interested in the seller's property. The original listing agent

    A. is a dual agent.
    B. cannot disclose to the buyer offers received on the seller's property while it was listed with him.
    C. cannot disclose to the buyer information about the physical condition of the property.
    D. cannot represent the buyer.

80. A real estate salesperson has been working with buyers. After she helps them negotiate, the buyers ask the salesperson if she can help them secure a mortgage. The salesperson knows a lender who pays a fee for referred buyers. Should the salesperson refer the buyers to this lender?

    A. No, this would be an unwise referral.
    B. Yes, if the salesperson and the buyers have previously entered into a written buyer agency agreement
    C. Yes, if the salesperson discloses the referral fee to the sellers
    D. Yes, if the lender offers the best interest rates and terms available in the market

81. A buyer contacts a real estate office and indicates an interest in purchasing a home in the area. Without entering into a buyer agency relationship with the buyer, a salesperson from the real estate office can do all of the following EXCEPT

    A. provide the buyer with information on properties for sale in the area.
    B. give the buyer rate sheets from several lenders.
    C. prepare a CMA on a home of interest.
    D. explain to the buyer about buyer agency, seller agency, and dual agency.

82. A buyer prospect working with one agent is interested in a house listed with an agent from the same company. Is this allowed in Illinois?

    A. Yes, but the buyer's agent becomes a dual agent.
    B. Yes, but the broker of the company is now a dual agent
    C. Yes, this is allowable.
    D. No, this is not allowable under Illinois license law.

83. A listing agent submits a listing to the local MLS. All of the following may follow MLS instructions and show the property without prior permission EXCEPT a(n)

    A. exclusive buyer's agent.
    B. nonexclusive buyer's agent.
    C. subagent.
    D. designated agent.

84. Buyer brokerage contracts in Illinois

    A. must be in writing to be enforceable.
    B. must be on specific forms.
    C. are not regulated under the license laws.
    D. are illegal.

85. All of the following provisions are included in the OBRE's rules regarding listing agreements EXCEPT

    A. a listing agreement must state the basis or amount of commission the broker will earn.
    B. a listing agreement must be accompanied by a qualified expert's report of the property's condition.
    C. a listing agreement must be signed by both broker and seller.
    D. the seller must receive a true copy of the listing agreement after signing it.

86. What types of agency exist in Illinois?

    A. Seller, buyer, undisclosed dual
    B. Seller, disclosed, dual, subagency
    C. Seller, buyer, disclosed dual, subagency
    D. Seller, buyer, full fiduciary

87. In a dual agency situation, a broker may collect a commission from both the seller and the buyer if

   A. the broker holds a state license.
   B. the buyer and the seller are related.
   C. both parties give their informed, written consent to the dual compensation.
   D. both parties are represented by attorneys.

88. A buyer is interested in seeing a house listed with XYZ Realty but does not discuss agency or buyer representation with the agent he is working with from LMN Realty. The LMN Realty agent can show the buyer the house and will

   A. by default, represent the buyer.
   B. represent the seller as a subagent.
   C. be a dual agent if so.
   D. The LMN agent may not show it.

89. A seller is required to give a buyer a real property disclosure report in all of the following transactions EXCEPT

   A. when the seller is not assisted by a licensed real estate agent.
   B. when the seller has not resided on the property in the last year.
   C. for a sale of commercial property.
   D. when the buyer has lived on the property as a tenant.

90. A real property disclosure report must be delivered to the buyer no later than

   A. the time that the buyer and seller sign a contract to purchase.
   B. the application for mortgage loan.
   C. the time of the home inspection.
   D. 24 hours before closing.

91. The seller has no knowledge of any plumbing system problems on the property she is selling. In actuality, however, the pipes are seriously corroded and will soon need to be replaced. In the seller property condition disclosure, when responding to whether the seller has any knowledge of plumbing system problems, she should respond

   A. "yes."
   B. "no."
   C. "unknown."
   D. The seller would not be required to respond to this question.

92. A broker lists a home and asks the seller to fill out a property condition disclosure. Which statement is true in Illinois?

   A. The disclosures are optional, and the seller may avoid liability by refusing to make any disclosures about the condition of the property.
   B. The standard disclosures only cover a narrow range of structural conditions.
   C. An agent should not give the seller any advice regarding which property conditions to disclose and which to ignore.
   D. Seller disclosure of known property conditions is required by statute.

93. Five years ago, Unit 5B in a condominium community was the site of a brutal and highly publicized murder. The unit was sold to an elderly woman who contracted the AIDS virus in a blood transfusion and died in the unit last year. As the agent for the woman's estate, what are your disclosure responsibilities to prospective purchasers of Unit 5B?

    A. You must disclose both the murder and the AIDS-related death.
    B. You are specifically prohibited by law from disclosing either event.
    C. You are specifically relieved of liability for nondisclosure of either event by Illinois license law.
    D. You do not need to disclose the murder, but you must disclose the AIDS-related death.

94. A broker took a listing for a small office building. Because the property is in excellent condition and produces a good, steady income, the broker's salesperson has decided to purchase it as an investment. If the broker's salesperson wishes to buy this property, the salesperson must

    A. resign as the broker's agent and make an offer after the owner has retained another broker.
    B. have some third party purchase the property on the salesperson's behalf so that the owner does not learn the true identity of the purchaser.
    C. obtain permission from the OBRE.
    D. inform the owner in writing that the salesperson is a licensee before making an offer.

95. Six months after the buyer bought a house, the roof leaked during a rainstorm. When the house was listed, the seller told the broker that the roof leaked, but they agreed not to tell any prospective buyers. The broker claims that the buyer did not ask about the roof. Under these facts the buyer

    A. can sue the broker for nondisclosure.
    B. cannot sue the broker under Illinois license law.
    C. can sue the seller under Illinois license law.
    D. has no legal recourse because the leaking roof could have been discovered by inspection.

96. A real estate licensee has signed a brokerage agreement with a tenant, who is looking for an apartment to rent. The licensee does not charge a fee to prospective tenants; rather, the licensee receives a commission from landlords. The licensee tells a landlord that the prospective tenant could probably pay a somewhat higher rent than the landlord is asking. Which of the following statements is true?

    A. The licensee owes the statutory agency duties to the landlords who pay the commission.
    B. The licensee's disclosure to the landlord was appropriate under these circumstances.
    C. The licensee's disclosure violated the statutory duties owed to the tenant.
    D. Because the licensee is not charging a fee to prospective tenants, the licensee has violated Illinois agency laws.

97. All of the following are exempt from the Real Property Disclosure Act EXCEPT a

    A. foreclosure sale.
    B. sale by a father to a son.
    C. conveyance of a primary residence from one former spouse to another under a divorce settlement agreement.
    D. sale by a real estate licensee of a two-unit residential property.

98. A licensed salesperson obtains a listing. Several days later, the salesperson meets prospective buyers at the property and tells them, "I am the listing agent for this property, and so I'm very familiar with it." Under these circumstances, and at this point, the salesperson

    A. has failed to properly disclose his or her agency relationship.
    B. has properly disclosed his or her agency relationship with the seller.
    C. is in violation of Illinois regulations, because the listing belongs to the broker.
    D. has created an unintended dual agency, which is a violation of Illinois regulations.

99. A real estate broker representing the buyer knows that the property has a cracked foundation and that its former owner committed suicide in the kitchen. The broker should disclose

    A. both facts.
    B. the suicide, but not the foundation.
    C. the cracked foundation, but disclosing the suicide could constitute a breach of duty to the client.
    D. neither fact.

100. The broker has entered into a listing agreement with the seller. Another broker, who has been working with a buyer, learns of the property through the MLS. Typically the second cooperating broker would represent

    A. the seller as a subagent.
    B. the buyer as an agent.
    C. the buyer as a subagent.
    D. neither buyer nor seller.

101. A broker decides to "sweeten" an MLS listing for a property by making a blanket offer of subagency. Is the broker's action acceptable?

    A. Yes, because Illinois law permits the creation of subagency relationships only through multiple-listing services
    B. Yes, because a subagency relationship may be created by either a blanket offer in an MLS or through a specific agreement between parties
    C. No, because subagency is illegal under Section 15 of the Real Estate License Act
    D. No, because subagency relationships in Illinois may be created only by a specific agreement between parties

102. In Illinois, what is the statutory usury ceiling on loans secured by real estate?

    A. 10 percent
    B. 15 percent
    C. 22 percent
    D. There is none.

103. Unclaimed estates escheat to the

    A. state in which the property is located.
    B. state in which the person died.
    C. county in which the person died.
    D. county where the property is located.

104. A couple with a five-year-old son lives in their own home in Illinois. Knowing their house contains some surfaces with lead paint, the couple had their son tested for evaluated blood levels, and the tests showed he had no lead in his system. Does Illinois law require that the parents take any action with regard to the lead paint in their home?

    A. Yes, they must abate all lead paint.
    B. Yes, they must abate defective lead paint.
    C. No, abatement is required only when the child has an elevated blood lead level.
    D. No, abatement of lead paint is not required.

105. A homeowner has a mortgage loan secured by real property. Under Illinois law, the homeowner may terminate the loan's escrow account when the remaining balance is equal to or less than what percentage of the original amount?

    A. 35 percent
    B. 50 percent
    C. 65 percent
    D. 75 percent

106. Twenty years ago, a homeowner obtained a 30-year mortgage loan to purchase a home. The interest rate on the loan was 9.275 percent. Today, the homeowner is prepared to pay off the loan early. Based on these facts, which of the following statements is true in Illinois?

    A. The homeowner's lender is entitled by statute to charge the homeowner a prepayment penalty equal to a year's interest on current balance of the loan.
    B. The homeowner's lender is permitted by Illinois statute to charge a prepayment penalty of up to 8 percent of the current balance of the loan.
    C. Illinois does not take an official statutory position on the issue of prepayment penalties.
    D. Because the homeowner's interest rate is greater than 8 percent, the lender may not charge a prepayment penalty under Illinois law.

107. All of the following are title search methods commonly used by an attorney in Illinois EXCEPT a(n)

    A. Torrens certificate.
    B. title search and opinion.
    C. certificate of title.
    D. abstract of title.

108. In Illinois, the responsibility for preparing any promissory notes involved in a closing belongs to the

    A. seller's broker.
    B. settlement attorney.
    C. lender.
    D. buyer

109. A sales contract is signed on May 1. Closing takes place on June 10, and the deed of trust is recorded on June 15. The borrower's first payment is due on August 30. When is the soonest that the broker receive his or her commission check?

    A. May 1
    B. June 10
    C. June 15
    D. August 30

110. In Illinois, who is responsible for calculating the prorations between the buyer and seller, searching the title, and preparing the mortgage note and deed prior to closing?

    A. Broker
    B. Salesperson
    C. Closing attorney
    D. Lender

111. The broker or salesperson may perform all of the following in preparation for the closing EXCEPT

    A. maintain a time schedule and provide data.
    B. explain closing procedures to both buyer and seller and arrange to have utilities transferred.
    C. coordinate inspections and deliver documents and escrow monies to the appropriate attorney.
    D. conduct any title searches that might be required.

112. A husband is survived by his wife and their two daughters. The couple's home is held in joint tenancy and is worth $50,000, but the husband has also left a separate estate worth $150,000. Because the husband died suddenly without leaving a will, the wife acquires

    A. sole ownership of the home and her daughters each receive $75,000 from the husband's separate property.
    B. sole ownership of all of the property and money.
    C. sole ownership of the home plus one-half of the separate property or $75,000. Her daughters split the other half or $37,500 each.
    D. sole ownership of the home plus one-third of the separate property or $50,000. Her daughters receive the remaining two thirds of the estate or $50,000 each.

113. A husband never made a will because he believed that wills brought bad luck. Last week, he was killed in a car accident. He is survived by his wife and two adult children. How is the husband's estate divided?

    A. All of the husband's estate passes to the wife.
    B. One-third to the wife and one-third each to the children
    C. One-half to the wife and one-quarter each to the children
    D. One-quarter to the wife with the remaining estate divided between the children

114. The decedent left an estate valued at $900,000, after the payment of all taxes and debts. She had no surviving husband, but three children. The first son died shortly after his mother did, leaving two children of his own, one of whom is adopted. The daughter has three children and the remaining son has two. The decedent did not write a will. How is her property divided?

   A. The daughter and remaining son each take $450,000.
   B. The daughter and the remaining son each take $300,000, and the first son's children divide the remaining $150,000.
   C. The daughter takes $300,000, the remaining son takes $300,000 and the natural born child of the first son gets the other $300,000.
   D. The estate will escheat to the state.

115. How old must a citizen of Illinois be before legally preparing a binding will?

   A. 15, as long as real property is not involved
   B. 18
   C. 21
   D. Any age as long as the will is legally witnessed and recorded

116. How many witnesses must sign in the presence of the person making a will to fulfill the legal minimum?

   A. One
   B. Two
   C. Three
   D. Four

117. A married couple, residents of Illinois, are co-owners of their home. If the home is sold in order to satisfy their unpaid credit card debts, how much will the creditors receive if the property sells for $165,000?

   A. Nothing–an IL resident's home may not be sold except to satisfy a mortgage debt or real estate taxes
   B. $150,000
   C. $157,500
   D. $162,500

118. How much of a homestead estate is an individual entitled to in his or her Illinois residence?

   A. $3,250
   B. $5,000
   C. $7,500
   D. $10,000

119. Which of the following legal life estates could be available to a surviving husband in Illinois?

   A. Homestead
   B. Dower
   C. Curtesy
   D. A marital easement

120. The method of describing property in Illinois that includes directions and distances is known as the

   A. colonial block grant system.
   B. system of principal meridians and baselines.
   C. system of metes and bounds.
   D. rectangular survey system.

121. The general datum plane referred to by surveyors throughout Illinois is the

   A. Chicago City Datum.
   B. New York Harbor Datum.
   C. United States Geological Survey Datum.
   D. Centralia Datum.

122. A straight line more or less connecting Rockford and Cairo is the

   A. Second Principal Meridian.
   B. Third Principal Meridian.
   C. Fourth Principal Meridian.
   D. Centralia Base Line.

123. All of the following legal descriptions are used in Illinois EXCEPT

   A. metes and bounds.
   B. the government rectangular survey system.
   C. lot and block.
   D. Torrens certificates.

124. A property located in the NW 1/4 of Section 10, Township 10 North and Range 2 West of the Third Principal Meridian would be located where in relationship to the initial point?

   A. Northwest
   B. Northeast
   C. Southwest
   D. Southeast

125. Which is NOT a proper legal description of real estate in Illinois?

   A. Section 12 of T 3 N, R 4 E, Third Principal Meridian.
   B. 203 N. Delane, Heyworth, IL.
   C. Lot 5, Block 2 of Sunset Acres Subdivision, McLean County, IL.
   D. a metes-and-bounds point of beginning at the northwest corner of Section 4, T 2 N, R 2 W, Third Principal Meridian.

126. How many principal meridians are located in Illinois?

   A. Two
   B. Three
   C. Four
   D. Six

127. A homeowner contracted with Super Construction Company to put a new deck on her house. They began work on May 1 and finished on June 1, but they were never paid. On July 1, the homeowner sold her house to a buyer, who received a mortgage loan from Country Bank and a mortgage loan from City Bank. City Bank recorded its mortgage on July 1. Country Bank recorded its mortgage on July 2. Super Construction Company records a mechanic's lien on July 3. What is the priority of the liens?

   A. Super Construction, City Bank, Country Bank
   B. City Bank, County Bank, Super Construction
   C. Super Construction, then City Bank and Country Bank equally
   D. City Bank and Country Bank equally, then Super Construction

128. For three days, a construction crew built an attractive gazebo in his back yard as the property owner watched. The owner had not contracted with anyone to build a gazebo and in fact had never given much thought to having one. But the homeowner liked what he saw. When the contractor presented the homeowner with a bill for the work, the homeowner refused to pay, pointing out that he'd never signed a contract to have the work done. Can the contractor impose a mechanic's lien on the homeowner's property under Illinois law?

    A. No, in Illinois a mechanic's lien attaches on the date the contract is signed or the work is ordered, and neither event occurred here.
    B. No, the homeowner cannot be forced to pay for the contractor's mistake.
    C. Yes, when a homeowner knows of work being done on his or her property and does not object or disclaim responsibility, a mechanic's lien may be created.
    D. Yes, however, the homeowner should have mailed a notice of nonresponsibility to the contractor's main place of business.

129. Once a judgement is rendered, a creditor on a judgment must enforce it within

    A. six months.
    B. one year.
    C. five years.
    D. seven years.

130. In Illinois, an individual may enter into legally enforceable contracts (with no exceptions) when he or she reaches the age of

    A. 16.
    B. 18.
    C. 19.
    D. 21.

131. If a minor enters into a contract in Illinois, what is the statutory period within which she or he may legally void the contract after reaching the age of majority?

    A. Six months
    B. One year
    C. The contract may be voided only up to the date when the minor reaches the age of majority; after that date, the contract is binding.
    D. There is no statutory period.

132. In Illinois, the prescriptive period to acquire an easement is

    A. 100 months.
    B. 12 years.
    C. 20 years.
    D. 30 years.

133. Acquisition of land by adverse possession requires use of land

    A. with the owner's permission.
    B. for a period of 30 years.
    C. privately so as to avoid being seen.
    D. without the owner's permission.

134. Which of the following is an example of a license, and therefore not entitled to a claim of adverse possession?

   A. A person who has been in possession of the property for 19 years
   B. A person who held the property for five years after "inheriting" it from a parent, who was in adverse possession for ten years
   C. A person who has been entering an orchard and taking apples every October since 1972
   D. A person who has been parking his or her car on a neighbor's property for 20 years without permission

135. A neighbor has a ten-foot easement through W's forested lot for the purpose of walking to the bank of the river. The neighbor widens the path to 14 feet to accommodate his truck so he can launch his boat. W is furious. Which of the following is true in this situation?

   A. The neighbor's original use was a right; W can do nothing.
   B. The new use is hostile, and if not stopped within 20 years, it could become an easement by prescription.
   C. The additional four feet is a reasonable extension of the original easement and must be granted.
   D. If the neighbor uses the extension for 15 years, the original easement is his by adverse possession.

136. In Illinois, the landlord may terminate the rental agreement if a tenant fails to pay rent within how many days of being served a written demand?

   A. 5
   B. 7
   C. 10
   D. 30

137. A couple has signed a lease requiring them to waive their rights to the interest earned from the security deposit, although required by law. This provision is

   A. unenforceable, thus making the lease invalid.
   B. unenforceable, but the lease is still valid.
   C. enforceable because all parties agreed to it.
   D. enforceable only for the term of the lease.

138. When should the landlord first present the rules and regulations for tenants of leased property?

   A. When the tenant first violates them
   B. When the tenant requests them
   C. At any time during the rental agreement
   D. At the time the tenant enters into the rental agreement or at the time the rules or regulations are adopted

139. How long must a landlord wait before he or she can raise rents to reflect a substantial increase in property taxes?

    A. Forever, because this is illegal
    B. Until the lease expires
    C. Four months
    D. Six months

140. A tenant leased an apartment in a 40-unit building. What percent interest must her security deposit earn?

    A. 2 percent
    B. 4 percent
    C. 5.25 percent
    D. A rate tied to the minimum passbook rate of the largest commercial bank in Illinois

141. A tenant skips out on his last scheduled monthly payment on a one-year lease. In this situation, the landlord may

    A. keep the tenant's belongings.
    B. sue the tenant for the back rent.
    C. do nothing because the lease is terminated.
    D. extend the lease automatically because the tenant gave no notice.

142. Which of the following leases is enforceable?

    A. An oral 15-month lease
    B. A written 5-year lease
    C. A written lease for less than 6 months
    D. An oral 24-month lease

143. How must a landlord handle a security deposit?

    A. They can be used only for residential units.
    B. Landlords must pay all tenants interest on their security deposits.
    C. At the end of the lease, the landlord cannot apply the security deposit to rent owed by the tenant.
    D. In a property with five or more units, the landlord must return the deposit to the tenant within 30 days of the end of the lease or provide an itemized list of why the money was withheld.

144. A broker works for weeks to put a transaction together as a dual agent. After depositing the earnest money in her escrow account, the broker learns that the buyer has been in a car wreck and cannot close. The broker hopes to be reimbursed for time, so he asks the buyer for half the earnest money before releasing the rest to him/her. Is this legal in Illinois?

    A. No, holding earnest money "hostage" is illegal.
    B. No, unless the broker can get the seller to agree to these terms.
    C. Yes, the broker is entitled.
    D. Yes, and the broker could also sue the buyer in court.

145. If a landlord wants to terminate a year-to-year tenancy in Illinois, how much notice must the tenant receive?

    A. 7 days
    B. 30 days
    C. 60 days
    D. 120 days

146. A landlord signs a lead-based paint disclosure indicating that he has never had his building tested for lead and has no actual knowledge of lead paint on the premises. He must also give the new tenant a

   A. federally mandated booklet and a ten-day opportunity to test for lead.
   B. ten-day opportunity to test for lead.
   C. federally mandated booklet.
   D. federally mandated booklet and an opportunity to test if he or she has children under six years in age.

147. During a crime wave, a tenant decides to install a burglar alarm in a rented house. Does the tenant need to inform the landlord?

   A. No, the tenant has full right of possession during the lease.
   B. No, only tenants in multi-unit apartment buildings are required to inform a landlord about a security system.
   C. Yes, but the tenant must also give the landlord instructions and passwords
   D. Yes, but the cost of the system may be deducted from the rent

148. A renter is on a month-to-month lease with rent due the first of each month. The tenant pays her rent on June 1, then decides on June 5 to move to a new apartment. If she gives her notice on June 5, when is her lease up?

   A. July 1
   B. July 31
   C. July 5
   D. August 5

149. How soon must deeds of conveyance be recorded after closing?

   A. A reasonable time
   B. One business day
   C. Three business days
   D. One month

150. In Illinois, the local official who records deeds and maintains the grantor/grantee lists is the

   A. first selectman.
   B. assessor.
   C. tax collector.
   D. county recorder.

151. In Illinois, if an owner defaults on his or her mortgage loan and the property is ordered sold at a foreclosure sale, the owner may redeem the property

   A. prior to the sale, under the statutory right of redemption.
   B. prior to the sale, under the equitable right of redemption.
   C. after the sale, under the equitable right of redemption.
   D. after the sale, under the statutory right of reinstatement.

152. If there is no redemption before the foreclosure sale, how long must a tax sale purchaser wait before action to obtain a tax deed?

   A. Two years after unpaid taxes are due
   B. One year from the date of the tax sale
   C. Three years from date of the tax sale
   D. Two years from date of the tax sale

153. How long is the defaulted borrower's redemption period after a foreclosure sale is complete?

    A. One year
    B. Six months
    C. Three years
    D. There is no redemption period.

154. The transfer tax levied by the state on the seller of the property is based on the

    A. selling price.
    B. earnest money.
    C. amount of the mortgage.
    D. time of the purchase.

155. How must the real property transfer tax be paid?

    A. By personal check, made out to the Department of Revenue
    B. By certified check, made out to the Housing Development Authority
    C. By purchasing transfer tax stamps from the county recorder
    D. By purchasing a "Green Sheet" from the county recorder for the total due

156. All of the following properties are exempt from paying general real estate taxes EXCEPT

    A. cemeteries.
    B. federal government buildings.
    C. housing owned by a disabled veteran.
    D. private schools.

157. How often is the assessed valuation of real estate in Illinois adjusted by county authorities?

    A. Quarterly
    B. Annually
    C. Biennially
    D. Every three years

158. In Illinois, real estate taxes become a lien on the property on

    A. January 1.
    B. June 30.
    C. July 1.
    D. December 31.

159. Except in Cook County, an Illinois property owner can pay the current year's real estate tax in two equal installments. The second half must be paid by

    A. June 1 of the current year.
    B. December 20 of the current year.
    C. January 1 of the next year.
    D. September 1 of the following year.

160. Outside of Cook County, real estate in Illinois is assessed at

    A. 16% of fair market value.
    B. 33⅓% of fair market value.
    C. 40% of fair market value.
    D. 100% of fair market value.

161. In Illinois, a reduction in real property tax for a personal residence may be available to all of these EXCEPT a

    A. 78-year-old retiree
    B. 26-year-old single parent
    C. 34-year-old man who has added a room addition
    D. 41-year-old woman who is renting the home.

162. A recently recorded deed states that the purchase price was "$10 and other good and valuable consideration." Tax stamps indicate $210.00 was paid for the state and county transfer tax. Assuming no mortgage assumption, what was the approximate price the property sold for?

    A. $10
    B. $140,000
    C. $105,000
    D. $210,000

163. What is the Illinois and county transfer tax on a property that sells for $250,000?

    A. $162.50
    B. $250.00
    C. $375.00
    D. $1,250.00

164. What is the county transfer tax on a property that sells for $190,000?

    A. $47.50
    B. $95.00
    C. $190.00
    D. $285.00

165. In Illinois, the market value of a home is $150,000. Of this amount, $25,000 is the value given to the land and $125,00 is considered "improvements." The owners have filed for their $3,500 homeowner's exemption, and it has been granted. The total tax levy on the property will be 7.750 per $100. How much will their real estate taxes be?

    A. $2,957.92
    B. $3,603.75
    C. $11,625.00
    D. $3,875.00

166. A house was sold for $150,000, with the buyers assuming a $40,000 mortgage. How much will the revenue stamps cost?

    A. $165
    B. $ 225
    C. $ 55
    D. $ 375

167. If a broker's violation of the license law results in monetary damages to a consumer, what is the latest date by which the injured party may file a lawsuit that results in a collection from the Real Estate Recovery Fund?

    A. One year after the alleged violation occurred
    B. Two years after the party became aware of the violation
    C. Two years after the alleged violation occurred
    D. Three years after the date on which a professional relationship of trust and accountability commenced

168. If an aggrieved person is awarded a judgment against a real estate licensee for violation of the Illinois License Act, which correctly states the aggrieved party's rights regarding the Real Estate Recovery Fund?

   A. Under Illinois license law, the aggrieved party has the right to immediately appeal to the OBRE for payment from the Real Estate Recovery Fund for the full judgment amount plus court costs and attorney's fees.
   B. The aggrieved party has the right to a maximum award amount of $50,000 from the Real Estate Recovery Fund, plus court costs and attorney's fees.
   C. The aggrieved party has the right to seek satisfaction from the licensee in a private civil action after being compensated from the Real Estate Recovery Fund.
   D. The aggrieved party has the right to a $10,000 maximum recovery from the Real Estate Recovery Fund.

169. All of the following are forms of joint ownership recognized under Illinois law EXCEPT

   A. tenancy in common.
   B. joint tenancy with survivorship rights.
   C. tenancy in severalty.
   E. tenancy by the entireties.

170. The purpose of the Illinois Real Estate Recovery Fund is to

   A. ensure that Illinois real estate licensees have adequate funds for continuing education fees.
   B. provide a means of compensation for actual monetary losses suffered by individuals as a result of the acts of a licensee in violating the license law or other laws in a real estate transaction.
   C. protect the Office of Banks and Real Estate from claims by individuals that they have suffered a monetary loss as the result of the action of a licensee's actions in a real estate transaction.
   D. provide an interest-generating source of revenue to fund the activities of the Office of Banks and Real Estate.

171. Whenever OBRE is required to satisfy a claim against a licensee with money from the Real Estate Recovery Fund, the

   A. licensee may continue engaging in real estate activities under the Commission's direct supervision.
   B. will immediately have their licensee revoked and must repay the full amount plus interest to the account if his or her license is ever to be reinstated.
   C. aggrieved party may later collect additional damages by forcing the sale of any property newly acquired by the defendant licensee.
   D. licensee must thereafter pay $25 per year into the account when applying to renew his or her license.

172. A broker commits a fraudulent act in connection with the sale of a property on March 15, 2001. On March 30, the transaction closes. On November 1, the client sues the broker, alleging fraud. On December 20, the jury finds in favor of the client. The client must file a claim with OBRE to recover money from the Real Estate Recovery Fund within

    A. 30 days following the illegal activity; in this case, by April 15, 2001.
    B. 30 days after having been awarded a judgment by the courts; in this case, by January 20, 2002.
    C. one year of filing suit; in this case, by November 1, 2002.
    D. two years of the date of closing; in this case, by March 30, 2003.

173. In Illinois, dower and curtesy are

    A. currently recognized.
    B. recognized voluntarily.
    C. recognized but not enforced.
    D. not recognized.

174. A husband and wife, who own their home as tenants by the entireties, obtain a divorce. At that time, the tenancy by the entireties

    A. extinguishes and becomes a tenancy in common.
    B. continues until one of them dies.
    C. extinguishes and becomes a tenancy at sufferance.
    D. reverts to common interest ownership.

175. To establish a "marketable record title," an unbroken chain of title must be established for a period of at least

    A. 15 years.
    B. 20 years.
    C. 40 years.
    D. 60 years.

176. Unless stated to the contrary in a deed, ownership of land by a married couple is assumed to be by

    A. severalty.
    B. joint tenancy.
    C. tenancy in common.
    D. tenancy by the entirety.

177. Why is 1997 a significant year in the history of title recordation in Illinois?

    A. The Torrens Act was repealed.
    B. All property that was registered under the Torrens Act was automatically transferred to the recordation system.
    C. Registration of new conveyances of real property under the Torrens Act ceased.
    D. Individuals may voluntarily change their property's registration from Torrens to the recordation system after that year.

178. A buyer enters into a purchase and sale contract to buy a house on October 15. The closing is November 15, at which time the seller delivers the deed. The deed is recorded on November 17. The buyer moves into the property on November 18. In Illinois, title passes from the seller to the buyer on

    A. October 15.
    B. November 15.
    C. November 17.
    D. November 18.

179. The husband owns a rental property occupied by a tenant. The wife has no ownership interest. If the husband wants to sell the property, who must legally sign the listing agreement and later deed?

    A. Both the husband and the wife because they are a married couple
    B. The husband only, because the husband and wife do not live in the house
    C. The husband as owner and the tenant in possession
    D. The husband, wife, and tenant

180. In Illinois, real estate brokers may place a lien against property for their commission based on the

    A. Real Estate Lien Act.
    B. Illinois license law.
    C. Illinois Lien Act.
    D. Commercial Real Estate Broker's Lien Act.

181. How many classroom hours must an Illinois real estate salesperson candidate take?

    A. 15
    B. 30
    C. 45
    D. 60

182. An Illinois salesperson wishes to get his broker's license. How many additional hours of education are required?

    A. 30
    B. 45
    C. 60
    D. 75

183. A broker in Illinois wishes to open three branch offices, but wants to keep her overhead costs down. How many additional branch managers MUST she have?

    A. None, she can manage all four offices herself
    B. One to manage all three branch offices
    C. Two, one to manage the home office and one for the branches
    D. Three, one for each branch office

184. A salesperson wants to form a corporation for the sole purpose of receiving commissions from her broker. Is this allowed?

    A. Yes, under some further guidelines
    B. Yes, as long as she is a broker and forms a real estate corporation
    C. No, not under Illinois law
    D. No, unless done by every agent in the office

185. A limited scope leasing agent license requires how many hours of classroom time?

    A. 30 hours
    B. 15 hours
    C. 45 hours
    D. 10 hours

186. A salesperson owns some rental homes that she advertises "For Rent" when they become vacant. She must follow all of these guidelines EXCEPT

    A. use a real estate company sign.
    B. put "agent-owned" on her "For Rent" sign.
    C. put "agent-owned" in her "For Rent" newspaper ad.
    D. not advertise in any company ads run by her sponsoring real estate firm.

187. A wealthy businesswoman wishes to hire someone to buy and sell all her Illinois property. Will this individual need an Illinois real estate license?

    A. No, as long as the individual just buys and sells for the owner.
    B. No, as long as the businesswoman has a license.
    C. Yes, buying and selling property requires a license.
    D. Yes, but only if the individual sells residential property

188. After failing the Illinois licensing exam three times, what would a candidate have to do to get three more tries?

    A. Take a 15-hour refresher course
    B. Take an advanced principles course
    C. Submit a new application and appropriate fee
    D. Complete entire education requirement again

189. An insurance agent wants to go into the real estate business. She wants to have her own office, so she will need a broker's license. Must she get her salesperson's license first?

    A. Yes, she must have a salesperson's license for one year.
    B. Yes, and once she receives her salesperson's license, she can immediately seek licensure as a broker.
    C. No, she must have one year's experience under another broker.
    D. No, she can go directly for the broker's license.

190. An agent is terminated by his broker for failure to pay the office bill. While the agent is looking for a new office, he or she is considered to have what kind of license?

    A. Inoperative
    B. Inactive
    C. Expired
    D. Conditional

191. An agent wishes to put up a huge billboard on the edge of town with his name and phone number on it. Must he also include his company's name as well?

    A. Yes, but the company's name must be the same size or larger than the agent's name
    B. Yes, as long as the company name is conspicuously displayed
    C. No, company names are no longer required.
    D. No, but the company phone number is required

192. An agent works for one real estate company, but then moves to a second company. Several transactions are pending during the move. Can the broker of the first company pay the agent directly after those closings?

    A. No, all compensation must come through employing broker.
    B. No, the agent gives up all commissions when leaving.
    C. Yes, commissions need not flow through the second broker.
    D. Yes, but the second company is entitled to a referral fee

193. Illinois agents are required by law to have

    A. E & O insurance.
    B. a separate and distinct office in their home.
    C. a written agreement with their broker.
    D. a car phone.

194. A licensed personal assistant wishes to hold an open house. Is this allowed in Illinois?

    A. No, assistants may not hold open houses.
    B. No, unless the house is vacant
    C. Yes, as long as the assistant's license is in a holding company
    D. Yes, if the assistant's license is held by the employing broker

195. All the following would be considered compensation to an agent in Illinois EXCEPT

    A. a thank you note.
    B. coupons or gift certificates.
    C. lottery tickets.
    D. a salary.

196. In Illinois, agents are required to disclose what kind of defects to a prospective buyer, regardless of who they represent?

    A. Patent defects
    B. All defects
    C. None, unless asked by the buyer
    D. Latent defects

197. All of the following can create buyer agency in Illinois EXCEPT

   A. the agent's actions.
   B. a written agreement.
   C. the agent's conversations.
   D. accepting subagency.

198. All of the following are statutory duties an agent owes a client in Illinois EXCEPT

   A. exercising reasonable skill and care.
   B. performing the duties of the brokerage agreement.
   C. following any instructions of the client.
   D. keeping confidential information confidential.

199. A buyer calls a licensee to see a new listing. Upon seeing it, the buyer wishes to buy it on the spot. The licensee insists that to do this, she must be a "dual agent." Is this correct?

   A. Yes, this is how it must happen.
   B. Yes, but the agent must get permission to be a dual agent
   C. No, the licensee should instead act as an agent for the seller and perform a "ministerial act."
   D. No, the buyer must be given all the agency options offered by the licensee's office.

200. A broker wants to open a real estate office inside his department store downtown. Will Illinois law allow this?

   A. Yes, if zoned correctly
   B. Yes, as long as she applies for a branch office license
   C. No, unless she gets city permission
   D. No, unless it is in a "separate and distinct" section of the building

ANSWER KEY

1. **B**

In Illinois, the Office of Banks and Real Estate administers the real estate license law. The Illinois Association of REALTORS® is a trade association. The Department of Housing and Urban Development is a federal agency that supervises housing issues.

2. **A**

The governor appoints the members of the Real Estate Administration and Disciplinary Board. They are not elected by the public or by real estate licensees.

3. **A**

The Office of Banks and Real Estate may suspend or deny a license for failure to pay taxes, child support, or any Illinois-guaranteed student loan.

4. **D**

New agents must have in their possession a sponsor card first, followed by a pocket card when the actual license arrives.

5. **A**

Apartment managers need to be licensed unless their primary residence is the apartment building being managed. Anyone holding a power of attorney has the authority to sign the principal's name and does not have to have a real estate license. Partners selling their own property are not required to have a real estate license.

6. **B**

In Illinois, a company that collects a fee for matching and assisting individuals who want to exchange properties requires a real estate license. Exempt from licensing requirements are resident managers who collect rent on an owner's behalf, MLS and advertising mediums, and executors or persons appointed by the court.

7. **B**

The agent already represents the seller. The agent becomes a buyer's agent (with or without a formal agreement) when showing the other listings. In coming back to the first listing, the agent is now a dual agent, which must always be disclosed and agreed to by parties.

8. **D**

The office coordinator is performing non-real estate activities and therefore is exempt from licensing requirements. The office coordinator is not necessarily the managing broker.

9. **A**

Sponsor cards are good for 45 days.

10. **C**

All of these are required, except being actively engaged as a licensed salesperson. This was a new development with the Real Estate License Act of 2000.

11. C
The buyer's agent must keep the lead-based paint form for five years.

12. D
The applicant has three years to apply for her license. This makes the date November 1, 2004.

13. D
The injured party must have had an active license at the time of the agreement. In fact, N might be guilty of practicing real estate without a license. Sponsoring brokers decide on filing suits.

14. C
The maximum fine is $25,000.

15. C
Salespersons' licenses expire on April 30 of odd-numbered years. (Brokers' licenses expire on April 30 of even-numbered years.)

16. D
Licensees must take 12 hours of continuing education every two years in order to renew their real estate licenses.

17. B
A licensee is given two years in which to reactivate his or her license once it has expired. After that, new course work must be completed and the state test retaken.

18. C
Generally, reciting published information is considered a ministerial act. Working directly with buyers, negotiating the merits of an offer, and assisting buyers in requesting repairs are all considered agent-level services.

19. C
Ministerial acts are services performed for a buyer that do not create an agency relationship.

20. C
Unlicensed assistants may not explain a contract to a buyer. Under the direction of a licensee, unlicensed assistants can perform simple bookkeeping activities, assemble legal documents, and prepare and distribute flyers and promotional materials.

21. B
Inserting factual information into forms under the agent's supervision is secretarial in nature and does not require licensing. Only licensed personal assistants may host open houses.

22. C
Illinois law does not allow protection periods for one-to-four unit residential property if the property is relisted by another agency. The first agent will get nothing.

23. C
Unlicensed assistants are not permitted to perform the described services. The broker and assistant are in violation of license law rules.

Illinois Exam Prep

24. B
While the applicant does not need to file an irrevocable consent to suit, he or she must be licensed in his or her home state. The applicant's home state must have the same or stricter criteria to obtain a nonresident license.

25. C
Resident (on-site) managers are exempt under the Real Estate License Act.

26. B
An individual who receives compensation for finding prospective buyers or renters must hold a real estate license. No license is required when acting on your own behalf. Resident managers are exempt from licensing requirements. A resident tenant who receives $1,000 or less, or the equivalent of one month's rent (whichever is lesser), with three referrals or fewer in any 12-month period, does not require a license.

27. D
One must successfully complete a course of 45 classroom, correspondence, or distance learning hours in general principles of real estate before applying for a real estate license.

28. B
Every broker's license expires April 30 of each even-numbered year.

29. C
Anyone engaging in the real estate business needs a real estate license. Individuals may, however, build their own houses without a license. A permit for construction is, however, usually needed.

30. D
The OBRE may revoke a license if the licensee has been convicted of a felony, false advertising, or commingling of funds. Commission rates are always negotiable between the seller and the broker.

31. D
Commingling of personal and client's funds is a strictly prohibited practice and is subject to disciplinary measures by the OBRE.

32. B
All would be considered grounds for suspension or revocation of license except properly depositing earnest money into the firm's trust account, which a broker routinely does.

33. B
A licensee would never be disciplined for negotiating a high commission, which as a businessperson he or she is free to do. Commingling funds or not performing as promised in a guaranteed sale plan could be grounds for suspension, revocation, or a hefty fine. Failing to provide information to the OBRE within 24 hours could also be grounds for discipline.

34. A
Continuing education instructors now receive hour-for-hour credit for the classes they teach.

35. B
The broker must always have permission before erecting a sign and must make full disclosure of all conditions of a promotion in the same ad or offer. Brokers are not permitted to solicit information or offer employment at the testing site and may not encourage a decision based on religious grounds.

36. D
All advertising is in the employing broker's name, and that name must be stated.

37. A
After obtaining permission, the broker may erect a "For Sale" sign on the property.

38. C
All advertising must state the name of the employing broker, not just indicate the licensee's box number or street address. A phone number is not sufficient identification. Advertising does not need to identify the property owner.

39. B
By law, the agent may sell "by owner", however, the contract with the broker may prohibit this. When acting as a private citizen, the salesperson need not disclose the broker's name in advertising, but would need to indicate that the property is "agent-owned" in advertising and on any "FSBO" yard sign.

40. A
Major screens or entrances to site sections must include the name of the brokerage, as well as the city and state of the principal office.

41. A
The salesperson must include city or geographic area for each property, the company name, and state of licensure if property is not within jurisdiction of his license.

42. B
Net listings are legal, but are discouraged because of potential conflict of interest for the broker and risk of fraud to the seller.

43. D
Commissions are always negotiable between the principal and the agent and are not set by law, local MLS, or local groups of brokers. Any price-fixing or talk of standard commissions is illegal under federal Anti Trust law.

44. A
Commissions are always negotiable between the principal and their agent and are not determined by custom or law. Commissions may not be shared with an unlicensed party and may be not be deducted from the earnest money deposit.

45. D
Other people's money must be deposited into a trust account within one business day after the final signature is obtained.

46. A
A broker does not have to open a new account for each earnest money amount received. However, the broker must keep careful records to accurately account for all funds, and they must be held in a federally insured depository. The account cannot be interest bearing unless both parties to the transaction agree to it. Trust monies must be in a different account, not necessarily in a different bank than the broker's bank.

47. B
The broker must deposit this buyer's funds into a special non-interest bearing escrow account (for money from customers and clients) within one business day after the final signature is obtained.

48. B
Real estate licensees who are not lawyers must be careful to avoid any appearance of the unauthorized practice of law. Blanks on preprinted form contracts may be filled in at the direction of the consumers who make final decisions and sign the contract. The broker and salespeople are special agents, hired for a very narrow purpose, which does not ordinarily include signing the name of the principal.

49. B
Listings must have an asking price, definite termination date, and a definable broker fee. An adequate description, such as the property address, is required, but this does not constitute the legal description. Legal descriptions are, however, both useful and necessary prior to the closing.

50. B
Listings must contain a definite termination date; rollover extensions are not permitted in Illinois.

51. B
Continuing education requirements are six hours of core courses and six hours of electives.

52. D
Other brokers are not required to participate in marketing, but the listing broker must give the seller a legible, signed, true, and correct copy. The participating MLS may require that the property be placed within 24 hours. Advertising is not required.

53. D
This type of offer is legal in Illinois if all the conditions are spelled out in the ad and there is no "tie" to special requirements made of the consumer (e.g., visiting a builder's sales office).

54. B
The licensee must pay a $50 fine and make the check good within 30 days or the license will be revoked.

55. C
Even though the broker claimed to be unaware of the salesperson's illegal activities, he or she can still be held responsible for the salesperson's license renewal deficiencies as this is something a broker should keep track of.

Illinois *Exam Prep*

56. B
Someone seeking a roommate can discriminate based on sex if they have to share a bedroom or bathroom.

57. B
Salespeople should be careful to avoid the unlawful practice of law by writing such a clause. Only a licensed attorney can prepare such a clause.

58. B
Salespeople may collect compensation only from their employing brokers.

59. D
Playing on the racial or religious fears of property owners to entice them to sell is called blockbusting and is a serious violation of fair housing laws.

60. B
The broker must sign the bottom of the license and give it to the agent, send one copy to OBRE, and keep one copy on file.

61. A
A salesperson may be licensed with only one broker, and may not hold concurrent licenses under or work for other brokers.

62. D
A salesperson may collect compensation only from his or her employing broker. Any bonuses that are received must go to the broker, who may at his or her discretion share them with the salesperson.

63. D
Agents' licenses are inoperative until "hired" by a new broker.

64. D
An office must be under the direction of a licensed real estate broker. A salesperson may not be named to such a post.

65. B
The office can be temporarily run by a sponsoring broker or under power of attorney for 30 days if OBRE is notified within ten days.

66. A
The broker may not offer a title opinion, which could be an unauthorized practice of law. In regard to the other answer choices, state law requires that all escrow records be retained for five years. The broker should make sure that all terms have been included; he or she is responsible for giving copies of documents to those that sign them.

67. D
In Illinois, a real estate office is not required to employ an additional salesperson since the broker could be the only "agent" in the office. Brokers are, however, required to maintain escrow account records for five years, keep both an escrow journal and ledger, and display a sign at the office location.

68. D
A broker may pay a referral fee only to someone who holds a real estate license. In this case, the broker can only say "thank you."

69. D
The OBRE may refuse to issue a license, may suspend, or may revoke a license of a convicted felon.

70. A
All commissions are negotiated between a broker and the client and must be stated in the listing agreement.

71. A
A binding contract may not be titled an offer to purchase.

72. C
The *Quinlan and Tyson* case helped define what an agent can and cannot do in regard to real estate contracts. The other elements listed are true but they were not defined by *Quinlan and Tyson*.

73. A
While the broker must be able to substantiate his offer to purchase and indicate all terms so that the seller is not surprised, he or she need not purchase until the 90 days is up. The broker must market the property normally unless the seller waives this right.

74. C
All written offers must be presented to the seller immediately, but the broker must give the buyers a copy of the offer. Earnest money must not be placed in a personal bank account. Completing a false, second purchase agreement for the purposes of obtaining a larger loan is prohibited under any circumstances.

75. B
While an exclusive buyer-agency agreement, exclusive-right-to-sell agreement, and multiple listing must be in writing, an open listing does not have to be in writing.

76. B
According to the Illinois Human Rights Act, the "no pets" policy does not apply to visually impaired persons with guide dogs.

77. A
In Illinois, the age of legal competence is 18.

78. C
While sexual preference is not a protected class under the Illinois Fair Housing Law, it could be (an in some locations has been) added at the local level.

79. B
While the original listing agent is now free to represent the buyer and is not a dual agent, confidential information gained from his listing agreement with the seller must remain confidential. His or her new role as buyer's agent must be disclosed to the seller; his or her old relationship with the seller must be disclosed to the buyer.

80. A
RESPA rules prohibit referral fees of this nature. Salespeople can only receive compensation from their employing brokers.

81. C
The licensee can provide the buyer with information on properties for sale in the area, give the buyer rate sheets from several area lenders, and explain agency to the buyer without an agency agreement; however, he or she should not prepare a CMA on a home of interest without one.

82. C
"Designated agency" allows buyer and listing agents from the same firm to represent different parties, without the broker becoming a dual agent.

83. C
An agent acting as a subagent of the seller is the exception; it is not legal to offer subagency through an MLS in Illinois. The other types of agents may show the property freely.

84. A
The buyer brokerage contract is an employment contract and must be in writing to be enforceable although no form is specified in the law. Buyer brokerage contracts are regulated just as listing agreements are.

85. B
A qualified expert's report on the property condition is not required for a listing agreement. However, listing agreements must state the basis or amount of commission and be signed by both broker and seller. The seller must receive a true copy after signing.

86. C
Seller agency, buyer agency, disclosed dual agency, and subagency exist in Illinois, although it would be rare to be a subagent since subagency is illegal within an MLS.

87. C
Both parties must give their informed, written consent to the dual compensation.

88. A
Illinois law under the License Act of 2000 presumes that you represent the person you are working with, in lieu of a written agreement.

89. C
Seller property disclosure forms are required in the transfer of one to four residential dwelling units, even when the seller has not resided on the property.

90. A
The buyer needs this information before agreeing to terms of a contract, so the real property disclosure report must be delivered no later than the time of the contract signing. It should be provided as early as possible. If it is provided after signing, a buyer's right of rescission regarding the contract sets in.

91. B
Because the seller has no knowledge of the plumbing problems at the present time, she should respond "no."

92. D
Property disclosures must be made for the sale of all one to four residential dwelling units. The agent should encourage the seller to be honest and disclose known problems. If advice is requested regarding what to disclose, the seller should talk to an attorney.

93. C
State law does not require stigmatized property disclosure (such as a highly publicized murder), and in those cases a listing agent should follow his or her seller's wishes. Under federal fair housing laws, disclosure of AIDS is prohibited without a definite seller directive, preferably in writing.

94. D
The salesperson will have to inform the owner in writing that the salesperson is a licensee before making the offer. The salesperson does not have to resign and should not use a third party. There is no need to involve the OBRE.

95. A
The broker is required by law to disclose any fact that would materially affect the buyer's decision to make an offer. The fact that the buyer did not ask is irrelevant. While the buyer cannot sue the seller under license law, he or she could sue under the Residential Real Property Disclosure Act.

96. C
Representation is determined by who does the hiring, not who pays the fee. The licensee owes a duty of confidentiality to the tenant who hired the licensee. The disclosure was a violation of license law.

97. D
The seller of a residential two-unit property is covered in the Real Property Disclosure Act. A foreclosure sale, a sale between family members, or from one spouse to another in a divorce are all exempt.

98. A
This is an inadequate disclosure. Agency representation is not about the property; rather, it is about an agent's duties and obligations to a client and a customer. In this example, the buyers do not know what their relationship is with the agent.

99. A

While Illinois requires the buyer's broker (or the listing broker) to disclose known, latent material defects like the cracked foundation, the law does not obligate an agent to disclose other "occurrences" like the suicide. However, most interpret that a buyer agent's duty of "reasonable skill and care" requires disclosure of almost anything he or she knows. For this reason, the buyer's broker should disclose both the cracked foundation and the suicide.

100. B

The broker is assumed to be representing the person with whom the broker is working. An Illinois MLS cannot offer subagency under the laws of the License Act of 2000.

101. D

Subagency relationships may now be created only with a specific agreement between the parties, and never for a listing advertised by the MLS. For this reason, subagency is now rare.

102. D

Usury indicates an exorbitant interest rate. Under Illinois law there is no legal limit on the rate of interest that a lender may charge a borrower. (For this reason, on land contracts and in other private financing situations in Illinois, rates often are higher than usual). Most Illinois mortgage loans, however, are under federal regulations, which **do** limit the interest rates.

103. D

Unclaimed estates escheat to the county in which the property is located.

104. D

Abatement is not required in Illinois, but disclosure of the test results must be made if the property is put on the market.

105. C

The remaining loan balance must be 65 percent or less before the homeowner can terminate the loan escrow account.

106. D

Because the original interest rate was more than 8 percent, the lender may not charge a prepayment penalty.

107. A

Torrens certificates are no longer used in Illinois. Current title search methods in Illinois include a title search and opinion, certificate of title, and an abstract of title.

108. C

The lender is responsible for preparing any promissory notes.

109. C

The soonest date is June 15. The broker receives the commission check when the deed is recorded and funds are disbursed.

110. C

The closing attorney is responsible for these activities.

111. D
A broker should not conduct a title search, which could lead to charges of practicing law without a license. However, the broker can provide data, set up the schedule, explain procedures, and coordinate all inspections and deliver documents.

112. C
As a joint tenant, the wife receives sole ownership of the home and one-half of the separate property or $75,000. Her daughters split the other half or $37,500 each.

113. C
The wife receives one-half of the estate and the remainder is divided equally between the children.

114. B
The daughter and remaining son each take one-third of the estate or $300,000, and the first son's children divide the remaining third.

115. B
In Illinois, the age of majority is 18.

116. B
Two witnesses must sign in the presence of the person making the will.

117. B
The creditors will receive $150,000; $7,500 per person is homestead protected.

118. C
An individual is entitled to $7,500 homestead exemption in Illinois.

119. A
Only a homestead life estate is available to a surviving husband in Illinois. Curtesy and dower are not recognized in Illinois.

120. C
A metes-and-bounds description includes directions and distances.

121. C
The U.S. Geological Survey Datum is the general datum plane used by Illinois surveyors.

122. B
The Third Principal Meridian more or less connects Rockford and Cairo.

123. D
The exception is the Torrens Certificate system. In 1997, all remaining Torrens registrations were transferred to the recordation system.

124. A
The property would be located northwest of the initial point.

125. B
A mailing address is not an adequate legal description. All of the other answer choices are legal descriptions.

126. A
In Illinois, there are two principal meridians: the Third Principal Meridian and the Fourth Principal Meridian. The Second Principal Meridian is located in Indiana, but is used to describe property in eastern Illinois.

127. A
The mechanic has 90 days to file the lien, which is effective as of the date construction was completed. Thus, the mechanic's lien is first, then the mortgage companies as recorded (City Bank, Country Bank).

128. C
When a landowner knows of work being done on his or her property and does not object or disclaim responsibility, a mechanic's lien may be created.

129. D
A creditor must enforce a judgment within seven years; it can also be renewed for an additional seven years.

130. B
Some exceptions may enable a 16-year old the right to sign certain contracts. However, the legal age with no exceptions is 18.

131. D
A contract signed by a minor may be voided anytime in the future; however, it must be voided within a "reasonable" time of reaching majority or it remains in force.

132. C
Continuous, open, and notorious use must be established for 20 years, although in some cases the period can be shortened.

133. D
In Illinois, the use must be "open and notorious" use for 20 years for someone to acquire land by adverse possession.

134. C
Entering the property for a specific reason (picking apples) is a personal right (a license), and it may be revoked at any time.

135. B
The new use is "hostile" and, if not stopped, could become an easement by prescription. W should consult an attorney.

136. A
The landlord may terminate the rental agreement five days after giving proper notice.

137. B
The provision is unenforceable, but the lease is still valid.

138. D
The landlord should present the rules when the tenant is entering into the rental agreement or whenever the rules are adopted.

139. B
The landlord cannot modify the rental agreement until it expires.

140. D
For rental properties containing more than 25 units, the rate of interest for security deposits is tied to the minimum passbook rate of the largest commercial bank in Illinois.

141. B
The landlord may sue the tenant for the back rent.

142. B
Only a lease of less than one year may be oral and still be enforceable. A lease for five years would have to be in writing to be enforceable.

143. D
In rental properties containing five or more units, the landlord must return the security deposit within 30 days of lease termination or provide an explanation of why the money was withheld. If the property has 25 or more units, the landlord must pay interest.

144. A
A broker cannot hold earnest money "hostage," and so he or she must return the money to buyer.

145. C
The landlord must give the tenant a 60-day notice.

146. C
The landlord must provide the booklet, but tenants are not given a special timeframe or opportunity for testing.

147. C
The tenant must notify the landlord of any burglary alarm installation and supply him or her with instructions and passwords.

148. B
Notice must be given by the start of the next lease period: notice on July 1 to terminate July 31.

149. A
Deeds should be recorded within a reasonable time; however, the sooner they are recorded, the better.

150. D
The county recorder records deeds and maintains the grantor/grantee lists.

151. B
The homeowner has the right of equity of redemption; i.e., to redeem the property before title passes to the foreclosing creditor.

152. D
A tax purchaser must wait two years from the tax sale before starting action to obtain a tax deed.

153. D
Unlike a tax sale, there is no redemption period after a foreclosure sale.

154. A
The conveyance tax is based on the sales price.

155. C
Tax stamps are purchased from the county recorder or registrar of titles. "Green sheets" is no longer an applicable term; the form filed is the "Illinois Real Estate Transfer Declaration."

156. C
A disabled veteran would have to pay tax on his house. Cemeteries, federal government buildings, and private schools are not taxed.

157. B
County authorities adjust the assessed valuation of real property annually.

158. A
Taxes are due by December 31 and become a lien on the property on January 1.

159. D
The second tax payment must be made by September 1 of the following year.

160. B
Assessments in Illinois are 33⅓% of fair market value, except in Cook County where there is a sliding scale starting at 16%.

161. D
Because the tenant does not own the home, she is exempt from receiving a reduction in real property taxes. Owners who actually live in the property are eligible for a homestead exemption.

162. B
The tax is $.75/500 or portion thereof. Reverse the procedures usually used; so multiply by sets of 500 and divide by the tax rate. $210 × 500 = $105,000, then divide by $.75 = $140,000.

163. C
The transfer tax is $375. $250,000 divided by 500 × $.75 = $375.

164. B
The tax is $95.00. $190,000 divided by 500 × $.25 = $95.00.

165. B
The real estate tax is $3,603.75. $150,000 divided by 3 = $50,000- 3,500 = $46,500 × .07750 = $3,603.75.

166. A
The revenue stamps will cost $165.00. ($150,000 - $40,000 = $110,000 divided by 500 × .75 = $165.)

167. B
The suit must commence within two years of when the injured party knew, or should have known, of the onerous act or omission.

168. D
An aggrieved person may recover up to $10,000 in actual damages together with court costs and attorney's fees. The maximum liability against the fund arising from the acts of any single licensee or unlicensed employee is $50,000.

169. C
Tenancy in severalty is ownership by one person or one corporation. Tenancy in common, joint tenancy, and tenancy by the entireties are all forms of joint tenancy recognized in Illinois.

170. B
The purpose of the Illinois Real Estate Recovery Fund is to protect consumers by providing a means of compensation for actual monetary losses suffered by the consumer due to a licensee's actions.

171. B
The licensee will immediately have his or her license revoked and must repay the full amount plus interest to get the license reinstated.

172. B
The client must file for the funds within 30 days of receiving a judgment; in this case, within 30 days of December 20, which would be January 20, 2002.

173. D
Curtesy and dower are no longer recognized in Illinois, but remain common in some states.

174. A
Tenancy by the entireties extinguishes upon the divorce and converts to tenancy in common.

175. C
An unbroken chain of title is usually at least 40 years.

176. C
If there is no special wording in the deed, ownership is assumed to be by tenancy in common.

177. B
In 1997, all remaining Torrens registrations were automatically transferred to the recordation system.

178. B
Title passes on delivery of the deed, which in this case is November 15.

179. B
Only the husband must sign the deed because the wife has no homestead rights unless she has lived in the property while they were married.

180. D
A broker may place a lien against a property for an unpaid commission based on the Commercial Real Estate Broker's Lien Act.

181. C
The education requirement for a salesperson's license is now 45 classroom hours.

182. D
The education requirement for a broker's license is now 75 additional hours.

183. B
A broker must now appoint a managing broker for each branch office, but it can be the same person. In other words, you no longer need a separate "broker" for each branch.

184. A
Agents may now form corporations for the sole purpose of receiving commissions.

185. B
A limited scope leasing agent requires 15 classroom hours.

186. A
Agents may not use a company sign on non-listed or non-office-managed homes. If a property is "agent-owned," that must be stated on any "FSBO" yard signs and in all newspaper ads and marketing materials.

187. A
Illinois exempts individuals who buy and sell property owned by their employers.

188. D
The candidate will have to complete the entire education requirement again after failing the exam three times.

189. D
Illinois law now allows anyone to directly seek a broker's license, without acquiring a salesperson's license first. This is new under the License Act of 2000.

190. A
The license is considered inoperative while the agent looks for a new office.

191. B
The law has changed. The agent's name can now be larger as long the company name is conspicuously displayed. There are no requirements for phone numbers.

192. C
Commissions can be paid directly to the agent unless the agreed-upon broker-agent contract prohibits it.

193. C
While most real estate firms will expect an agent to secure E & O insurance, an agent is not required by Illinois law to have E & O insurance (nor a home office or car phone). He or she must always, however, have a written agreement with his or her broker.

194. D
A personal assistant may hold an open house if his or her sales license is held by an employing broker.

195. A
Anything of value (coupons, lottery tickets, gift certificates, salary) are considered compensation; the thank you note is the exception.

196. D
Agents are required to disclose unseen (latent) material defects to a prospective buyer, regardless of who they represent.

197. D
Accepting subagency does not create buyer agency. In fact, the opposite is true because subagents (where allowed) represent the seller while working with a buyer. Agency can be created by the agent's actions, by written agreement, or by the agent's conversations.

198. C
The agent must exercise reasonable skill and care, perform the duties of the brokerage agreement, and keep confidential information confidential. The agent may not follow "any instruction" of the client because the agent may follow instructions only if they are legal.

199. D
The buyer should be given his or her agency options. Under these circumstances, the licensee can continue to represent the seller and work with the buyer as an unrepresented customer.

200. D
The broker may open an office in his department store only if it is a "separate and distinct" area.